FUNCTIONS OF A SUCCESSFUL PROJECT MANAGER

FUNCTIONS OF A SUCCESSFUL PROJECT MANAGER

PREM VARDHAN

Notion Press

Old No. 38, New No. 6
McNichols Road, Chetpet
Chennai - 600 031

First Published by Notion Press 2017
Copyright © Prem Vardhan 2017
All Rights Reserved.

ISBN 978-1-947202-01-6

This book has been published with all reasonable efforts taken to make the material error-free after the consent of the author. No part of this book shall be used, reproduced in any manner whatsoever without written permission from the author, except in the case of brief quotations embodied in critical articles and reviews.

The Author of this book is solely responsible and liable for its content including but not limited to the views, representations, descriptions, statements, information, opinions and references ["Content"]. The Content of this book shall not constitute or be construed or deemed to reflect the opinion or expression of the Publisher or Editor. Neither the Publisher nor Editor endorse or approve the Content of this book or guarantee the reliability, accuracy or completeness of the Content published herein and do not make any representations or warranties of any kind, express or implied, including but not limited to the implied warranties of merchantability, fitness for a particular purpose. The Publisher and Editor shall not be liable whatsoever for any errors, omissions, whether such errors or omissions result from negligence, accident, or any other cause or claims for loss or damages of any kind, including without limitation, indirect or consequential loss or damage arising out of use, inability to use, or about the reliability, accuracy or sufficiency of the information contained in this book.

Contents

Preface . . . . *ix*

PROJECT MANAGER

Introduction. 3

1.0 Definition of a Project Manager 5

    1.1 Life Is a Project 7

2.0 Selection of a Project Manager. 13

3.0 How to Be a Successful Project Manager 17

    3.1 Honesty 19

    3.2 Enjoys Management Trust and
        Regularly Follows MIS Reporting 24

    3.3 Good Knowledge about the Project's
        Main Functions and Basic Knowledge
        of Its Support Functions 41

    3.4 Dedication to Duty 43

3.5 Human Resource Management 43

3.6 Planning and Foresight 44

3.7 Cost Consensus 47

3.8 Quality Conscious 48

3.9 Negotiation Skills 49

3.10 Decision-Taking Abilities. 51

3.11 Emergencies and Crisis Management. ... 52

3.12 Team Building 53

3.13 Presentable and Able to Converse with Clients and High-Profile People 57

4.0 Some Management Stories 61

    4.1 Innovation 62

    4.2 Planning. 64

    4.3 Emphasis on Human Resource Development. 67

    4.4 Keeping Abreast of the Latest Updates, Conducting Workshops Frequently to Keep the Team Updated with the Latest Advances. 70

    4.5 Pricing (in Major Contracts for Execution of a Project). 72

    4.6 Relationship with Subordinates 81

    4.7 Distribution of Duties to Juniors and Making Them Responsible for It 82

4.8 Relationship with Colleagues 83

4.9 Relationship with Seniors 83

4.10 Importance of Controlling Stress and
Avoiding Work Fatigue 85

4.11 Public Relations 87

4.12 Quality Assurance 88

4.13 Health, Safety and Environment 89

4.14 Business Development................. 92

4.15 Hierarchy............................ 93

4.16 Incentive 93

Preface

A leader is responsible for work done by a group of people and others in the group follow him. This leader gains such status not by birth but by continued efforts to excel in small or big assignments allocated to him. Successes make him more confident and reliable, to handle even bigger projects. He gets basic education by classroom lessons but he learns to implement the knowledge by experience and guidance. His actions and decisions are responsible for progress in his life and career.

Most failures are due to ignorance which could be avoided by proper understanding and guidance. Leaders also learn from failures and make sincere efforts not to repeat mistakes.

This book tries to highlight the expectations from a leader in many functions of his life and career, in minute, conceptual detail for better understanding and to help create a successful leader or project manager of any project or assignment.

Others in a team should not remain complacent but aim higher so that with strong will power and understanding, they would be able to, if not supersede, come second or third to the leader. True leaders are delighted when their disciples do better than themselves.

Prem Vardhan

vardhanprem@yahoo.com

PROJECT MANAGER

Introduction

Everybody undergoes a process of learning to manage his/her work assignments. In this process, every success takes them one step forward in their career and each failure sees them backtracking, depending on the gravity of the failure. One should learn by analyzing reasons for success and failure and avoid actions that might cause failures in the future. Most failures are due to ignorance or lack of knowledge and could be avoided by proper training and understanding the subject and seriousness in taking decisions to become a successful person or manager.

The Prime Minister of a country like India is the manager of the country's affairs, but the President is not. The President of India monitors the work of the Prime Minister to ensure he and his teams are working as per the constitution and in the general interest of the country. The President does not have any Executive Powers in India.

The President of the United States of America is also a manager, responsible and accountable for his/her country's affairs.

This book deliberates on the functioning and progress of managers at senior levels; all the issues discussed might not be applicable to an individual at a junior level. Instead of becoming nervous, one should concentrate on issues applicable now and wait for future ones as and when wider responsibilities are available/gained.

For executives in public life, this book considers the **government** as *owner* and the **public** as *client*.

Every responsibility has a corresponding accountability. Responsibilities are always earned and taken, but very seldom provided. One could take responsibilities to any limits, even beyond the horizon, depending on one's capability and interest.

1.0

Definition of a Project Manager

Work or a collection of works, within a defined scope, to be done in any walk of life could be considered a project. A project manager is the leader of group of people doing the said work.

Many organizations provide fancy designations as per the size of a project and offer promotions to keep employees motivated. However, the responsibility of the executive managing the project is the same for all positions. Designations could be section-in-charge, resident manager, resident director, managing director or many more.

A project is assigned to a project manager with a defined scope and parameters and he should work within these parameters in the best interest of the project. As an example, a project manager is expected to take clearances from seniors on certain issues like financial matters. This does not mean he is not responsible for the financial implications of his assignment, unless he has been told not to interfere in finance matters for some specific reasons. If he begins to think that "since I have not been given requisite powers, I need not worry about costs," he will never be given financial powers and may not even get section head status on future assignments. Financial powers are withheld not because the management does not trust you, but the management feels that you are not mature or capable enough.

If a person remains cost conscious and vigilant and continues to present proposals with recommendations for the best alternatives for execution on certain issues, management will accept such recommendations. Otherwise, management would explain why they considering his second-best recommendation. In the process, he learns a few more things and gains management confidence.

If he continues to give sensible proposals, management develops more confidence in his individual capabilities and would consider giving him better opportunities as and when these arise. Management waits for him to finish the work in hand before a better opportunity is provided. Such decisions are not taken in haste.

1.1 Life Is a Project

Life is a project and there are three ways to manage it:

1. A person who takes decisions himself without accepting others' interference and not interfering with others is **project manager of his own life.**

2. In matters pertaining to one's education, career and other important issues, decisions are taken by the head of the family. Hence, **someone else is the project manager for his life.** For example, in an affluent family, a family manager directed the children of his older brothers not to have more than a child each, for financial reasons, and everybody obeyed religiously. He himself had just one daughter.

3. A person who takes decisions for others in the family, decides on major issues in the family and is responsible for his decisions. The family trusts him and abides by his decisions, good or bad. Hence, he is **the project manager of the well-being of others in the family.**

1.1.1 A person who takes his own decisions

People, who take their own decisions, are very successful in their life and career as *project managers*. They

- Understand problems
- Analyze these problems

- Are aware that they would be solely responsible for their decisions
- Make satisfactory decisions or else try to improve
- Do not interfere in others' work unless it is called for
- Might consult with a few associated with the subject but will ultimately make decisions themselves
- Provide opportunities to their subordinates and kids to learn to take their own decisions in life.

Often their attitude becomes dictatorial, which is not correct and hampers further progress, as the possibility of taking wrong decisions increases. They must control their ego. It should not be surprising if ego is the reason for the start of his/her downfall. Such people start taking spontaneous wrong decisions and force them on others in the team. This is wrong and suicidal.

1.1.2 A person for whom somebody else takes decisions

People who lack confidence, knowledge and foresight in their youth often rely on the head of their family to take decisions for them. **They are content with decisions taken by the head of their family and live an easy life.** Some try and work quietly for their own existence and betterment. They are very good professionals but unfortunately not good managers. Some are very good doctors, engineers, businessmen and other professionals working at the second level and gladly accept their juniors becoming their project/reporting managers. Such people are not interested in taking additional responsibilities and are content where they are.

This generally happens if parents have a dictatorial attitude with children or favor and promote a specific child in the family to be the leader, neglecting others.

1.1.3 A person who takes decisions for others in the family

A family manager, among other things, is:

- A well-wisher and takes care of the whole family as per their status and requirements, without doing anyone any special favors
- The main member of the family, responsible for the growth and smooth functioning of business and domestic affairs
- Not self-centered
- Intelligent and capable of taking the right decisions
- Not likely to make biased decisions
- Someone whom all the family members trust and who takes care of them

- A good manager of funds and spends within a budget as per earnings, taking care of the reasonable requirements of all family members
- Equipped with good foresight and has contingency plans for distress/emergencies
- Unlikely to become nervous in case of calamities and paves the way to everybody's satisfaction
- Able to distribute business and house work as per the capabilities of individual family members.

Such persons are very good project managers and execute their projects efficiently, assigning responsibilities to their associates/subordinates as per their capabilities and satisfaction. Even executives interested in working in their own style are welcome and a mini project is created for them with proper reporting structures.

Such people are competent and can handle large projects since they can manage a large group of executives.

Even in games like **cricket**, the team captain is the project manager and he assigns jobs to his teammates as per their capabilities and to everybody's satisfaction. **The captain commands the game played by his team, a well-knit group that works as a unit. It is not necessary that the captain be the best player of the team.** The captain must take care of the performance of the entire team and if the team does not perform well, he must, without losing patience and getting nervous, give his best and very often tilt the game in his team's favor by making a few on-the-spot changes.

The basic qualities and performance of project managers of all professional projects are alike even if different nomenclature is used for designations in different types of projects.

2.0

Selection of a Project Manager

'Chanakya' was a renowned Indian scholar and a teacher to Maurya Emperor Chandragupta. Chanakya picked up a child from the streets and trained him to become the emperor. For Chanakya, giving the kingdom an efficient emperor was a self-assigned project. **Chanakya was an accomplished project manager.**

A good project manager must have a good track record of performance in previous assignments as well as good leadership qualities.

His superiors have confidence that he has acquired the necessary skills while working in junior positions. He is given an opportunity that is denied to other project managers. His superior takes a big risk; if his project manager fails to perform as expected, not only is he denied further key responsibilities but his superior could face humiliation from his superiors in the management.

If the project manager succeeds in his first few assignments, it is his success but if he fails, it is the failure of his boss, who selected him. The boss is blamed for the unsatisfactory performance of the project manager; the project manager might only be demoted but his boss may even lose his job.

To save the project and his own prestige, the boss may change the project manager quickly or get himself involved in the project management. There is no point in blaming the boss for becoming difficult, since he must care for the project and not an individual. He gives an opportunity but if the individual does not perform, the boss must take corrective measures fast.

Even at the highest level, if a government is not performing well, the prime minister may change a few ministers or secretaries. If he is not able to improve performance even then, either the prime minister is changed by the party high command or the whole government is changed. **There cannot be a compromise on quality and quantity of work derivatives due to an individual, at any level.**

However, if the project manager succeeds to the satisfaction of management in his first few jobs, he is given bigger and more challenging assignments as project manager and often, the sky is the limit for his achievements. However, a sword is always hanging over his head, warning of dire consequences in case of failures, throughout his career and he must always work hard.

Many project managers draw so much respect that their word becomes the rule, but they should not become complacent and egoistic. Their downfall is generally only due to such obvious reasons and it is very quick.

Being egoistic is a situation where a person loses the ability to differentiate between good and bad and thinks that whatever is said by him/her is correct without paying heed to suggestions by well-wishers. He even takes decisions spontaneously without much thought and makes more mistakes.

Progress in career is entirely dependent on performances but if a performance is unsatisfactory, demotion might follow and it might be difficult to rise again to the same level. This is why somebody in a very coveted position in his professional, business or political career just vanishes in no time due to some silly mistakes.

3.0

How to Be a Successful Project Manager

A project manager must concentrate on many functions and take decisions as necessary. He has specialists for most functions, but should still check their work and give them advice/instructions for good performance of the project. He should have basic knowledge of all subjects. His analytical approach, decision-making capabilities and self-confidence are motivators for the team and contribute to the smooth implementation of the project. In addition, if the team realizes the supremacy of the project manager's knowledge and approach, they start respecting him and cooperate.

Such qualities and capabilities do not come on their own but are gained slowly by taking decisions on smaller problems. **Such decisions are not always correct** but dedication and seriousness in approach are important considerations. At the same time, such mistakes should be few, must be owned up to and never repeated.

Any development-oriented organization maintains a good record of the performance of all employees and a few are put on the fast track. All performance reviews have a column that indicates whether an employee has the potential to reach a certain level in the organization. After considering the views of a few senior executives connected with their work, deserving employees are put on the fast track for development. Such employees are given more opportunities to take critical decisions and sent for short-term management training courses. These employees are continuously judged on certain basic qualities including the following:

1. Is honest
2. Enjoys management trust
3. Rigorously follows Management Information System (MIS) reporting
4. Is knowledgeable about the project's main functions and support functions
5. Is dedicated to duty
6. Is capable of human resource management

7. Demonstrates planning and foresight
8. Is cost and quality conscious
9. Has negotiation skills
10. Has decision-making abilities
11. Can deal with emergencies and manage crises
12. Is capable of team building
13. Is presentable and can converse with clients and high-profile people.

3.1 Honesty

3.1.1 Honesty in money matters

Honesty in money matters is very important for the project manager, but this is a very complex subject in today's world. There are certain guidelines and expectations of the management in such matters and the project manager should perform within such guidelines and expectations to maintain the management's trust.

3.1.2 A contract-like arrangement with head office/owner of company

There are some organizations who pay a very low salary, to sustain and have an understanding with the project manager, so that he earns a certain fixed sum for the head office and the rest is the freewill of the project manager and his team, depending on how they manage the project. Likewise, a project manager and his team also develop some ambitions and after taking away such sums, very little is left to be spent on the project. With this, if the contract price is competitive, quality of work becomes substandard because corners are cut wherever possible and often, a project is left half finished.

It is difficult for such project managers to work further in any other financial arrangement nor would other organizations trust them and give them responsible positions. Such things are never a secret and news spreads very fast. A sensible, rising executive should avoid taking such assignments.

3.1.3 Government-project management

There are many cases where a minister tells the departmental secretary or managing directors of government organizations to arrange funds against government guarantees and get new projects executed through contractors, keeping a certain provision for the ruling party. In such cases, good development work is done in the state/country, but the government spends little extra money on all the contracts.

This works very well if the projects are planned such that they contribute to the development of the economy and the state can repay loans to financial institutions on time, maintaining strict discipline on repayment schedules.

For example, **if a commercial complex is built with thirty years' soft loan. The rental of the complex**

must be sufficient to pay back the loan, including interest, in a maximum of twenty to twenty-five years and the complex would be a free asset with the government thereafter. Similarly, power stations, industries and highways pay back the money invested by selling power, industrial products and charging toll tax from vehicles.

In one of the most practical arrangements, a contractor's project manager sells projects necessary for the country, for the development of his business. He prepares a project summary with benefits and cash flow for expenses and revenue generation for the perusal of authorities and convinces them that this project is good for implementation and would not be a burden but an asset to the government.

A project manager who knows all relevant details is better placed to win a contract, when a project tender is floated.

In at least sixty percent of government contracts, some organization interested in a part or full contract gets actively involved in the preparation of tender documents, specifications and conditions. Tenders are drafted as per their requirements, since they provide concepts and know-how and hence stand a better chance of winning their portion in the contract.

- The minister provides government guarantees.
- The secretary arranges funds.

- The contractor prepares a techno-commercial proposal as a business development initiative.

Many politicians have a fixed appetite to generate funds for their political party and the greater the number of projects, it's better distributed. There will be less load on individual projects.

It is often seen that one province progresses well while its neighbor stands still. Only a few projects are available to execute and everybody wants the lion's share and this causes the project to become a non-starter.

3.1.4 A honest project manager should not make illegal money for himself

This is a very common and necessary requirement in private organizations. They are generally willing to pay salaries as expected by the project manager and others. It is very simple: we trust you and are willing to pay you directly to cater for all your requirements including savings, but you are not to earn by unfair means. If this trust is shaken, they pull out the project manager from the project without giving any reason or justification.

It should be well understood that nobody is indispensable in this world. The author has worked as an employee for more than fifty-three years in very responsible positions but nobody ever felt that he was indispensable. It may be that this is the secret of his long innings in his profession.

It is a universal fact, which could be tested in many ways, that honesty and sincerity starts from the top. If the boss of the project is honest, impartial and vigilant, the entire organization reporting to him would follow in his footsteps and be honest. Someone might steal, but not for long and the moment he is exposed or doubts on his integrity are confirmed, he should be sacked without a second chance or any other consideration.

A story is told of a corrupt person in a kingdom who used to harass everybody for money. The matter was reported to the king. The king asked the man to sit on the sea shore and count waves. He started asking the people on incoming boats for money since they were disturbing the waves and creating a problem for him to count. Then the king asked him to count the stars at night. He started shouting at people who were asleep, since their buildings were obstructing his count of the stars. The king had to keep him around in accordance with the prevailing practice of the time, but these days, the project manager or the company generally is not under any compulsion to maintain such people.

Such a corrupt person could be important to the management. Hence, the project manager should not ask for the said person to be removed from the organization but only from the project. Certain people are kept for a short duration for some specific reasons, but making illegal money is not tolerated and such people are politely shifted to other assignments not involving financial dealings.

3.1.5 Honesty in decision making

The project manager is the head of the project and must take decisions in all matters related to the project, including human resource, administration, finance and procurements. He reports to senior management about project performance and some specific and critical decisions taken by him.

There are many issues brought to the project manager for approval with recommendations from functional managers. These issues are to be seriously considered, scrutinized and discussed at length with support staff and decisions must be taken in keeping with consensus and without any favors. It is not necessary for the project manager to approve proposals recommended by juniors.

If a project manager starts favoring any individual, it has an adverse effect on the team and they start losing respect for the project manager.

3.2 Enjoys Management Trust and Regularly Follows MIS Reporting

Once a project manager is appointed for a project, the owner bestows his trust on him although the owner is simultaneously worried about the performance of the project and the project manager.

The owner provides the client bank guarantees and insurance policies for project performance, valued at more than double the value of the project before the start of the project itself. In case of non-performance or non-completion of the project within the expected time or to the expected quality, he carries the risk of encashment of these guarantees by the client. The client could recover money from financial institutions that have provided such guarantees on behalf of the owner. In addition, the owner loses the reputation of his company and risks a drop in future jobs in case of non-performance and encashment of guarantees.

It is the duty of the project manager to correctly update the owner about project progress to reassure the owner. He should regularly provide the following information or any other information required by the owner, to him or his nominated representative:

1. Technical/system performance, actuals v/s expected
2. Physical performance, actuals v/s planned
3. Commercial performance, actuals v/s planned
4. Cash flow performances
5. Health, safety and environment protection, compliance and achievements
6. Quality and standards, compliance and achievements
7. Additional business prospects in the region

8. Any specific achievements

9. Any specific problems

Based on performances on the above parameters and any others specific to the project, the owner decides on whether to continue with the project manager. Good performance results in an increase in duties and more confidence bestowed on the project manager.

3.2.1 Technical/system performance, actuals v/s expected

How one starts and executes a project is very important. All jobs require certain technical or system innovations, developments and implementations. This is the primary requirement. **Even the implementation of well-defined and trusted systems in true perspective is a challenge and any improvement by innovation and development is always acclaimed**. This is the first test the project manager and his team must go through. Quality and sustainability of systems to be implemented on the project is key for the successful execution of any project. Progress on such developments and their implementations should be part of MIS reporting.

Sometimes there are incidences of failure and setbacks. Any wise project manager would change his approach on receiving the first signal of something going wrong, with ultimate caution and planning and without wasting time. Thus, successfully reversing possible failure. He should not hesitate to consult some experts in the field for corrective measures. If such incidences are reported to the management, they would support instead of ridiculing the project manager and try to help by giving sensible suggestions.

A group of ants carry a piece of food from the ground to the roof of a building, climbing a vertical wall. One could create many obstructions on their path. **The ants will fall again and again owing to such obstructions but ultimately, they will still climb to their destination by taking a detour. If ants can do it, then why can't humans?**

3.2.2 Physical performance, actuals v/s planned

Work on a project should be executed as per expected plans, systems and time schedules. Implementation/execution is always planned to be completed within a given timeframe. MIS reporting should include how much work has been executed in the specific time of reporting against planned progress. In cases of shortfall in progress, remedial measures should be suggested/sought in MIS reporting.

3.2.3 Commercial performance, actuals v/s planned

Any activity or job has some commercial value and efforts could be converted in terms of money spent and gained. The work or project makes profit if gains are more than the value spent. An organization spends time or energy that could be converted into money, for getting paid or as rewards for work executed.

Any project should have continuous commercial gains as the work progresses. These are commercial gains and not cash flow; both are different. Before the project starts, there should be planning for commercial performance in different stages and these performance actuals against planned should be reported in the MIS. Due to some unavoidable circumstances, time slots could have negative commercial performances. Such eventualities should be highlighted in project planning and in MIS reporting.

These performances are submitted in a tabulated form called performance statement. All project activities are highlighted as a statement of activities and depending upon quantum of work in each activity, a number is assigned to each activity, representing the cost of that activity. The sum of these numbers should be equal to the total cost of the project. This is called Work Breakdown Structure (WBS) statement.

These numbers are fed to the project time schedule in planning stage for all activities, to get a statement on how much the project cost would be for each month or any other reporting interval, if work is executed as per schedule. This planned schedule is tabulated and progress is reported in terms of actual costs v/s planned.

3.2.4 Cash flow performances

On most projects, certain expenses are incurred by the contractor in the purchase of materials, tools and in the mobilization of manpower. These expenses are like an investment and are recovered slowly through contribution from work bills. However, often, the client provides advances to cover such expenses and recover from work bills. In short, either the contractor or the client provides cash to cover the initial costs of the project, generally termed as **mobilization money or investment**. The return of this mobilization money and expected profits are to be made by the project in a planned manner from proceeds of periodical billing to the client or sales of products. This cannot be done abruptly at any stage of the project and even induction of funds is to be done slowly, as per requirement. Some projects are planned with initial aggressive billing to reduce induction of cash into the project.

Consolidation of all parameters of costs and revenues on a periodical basis, say monthly or fortnightly, is done by making statements for expected inflow and outflow for the duration of the project. These statements are tabulated together and an indicative pulse of the movement of money to and from the project is obtained. This is called the cash flow of the project.

The project cash outflow and inflow are planned strategically before the start of the project and variances if any in planned and actual cash flow are essential parts of MIS reporting.

The cash flow of a construction project would generally have the following division of costs, preferably broken down into cost heads for each month:

Inflow (Revenue)

- Initial support in the form of money from the client or owner, distributed, as planned, for each month for the duration of the contract
- Revenue/work bills for each month, as planned
- Less recovery of initial support money (as planned in stages)
- Less recovery of retention money, etc. from work bills
- Release of retention money by client
- Tax Deducted at Source (TDS)
- Net monthly inflow distributed for the duration of the project.

Outflow (Expenditure)
Fixed costs

- Costs of mobilization, including infrastructure, manpower, temporary camp facilities, etc.
- Capital purchases, like furniture, office and other equipment

- Project-specific equipment to be written-off on the project
- Purchase of know-how, consultant fees, computer programs, etc.
- Office and residential premise rentals
- Health, safety and environment costs
- Electricity, water and security
- Insurance

Variable costs related to progress of work

- Procurement of consumables
- Salaries and wages
- Bonus and gratuities
- Incentives
- Cars and other conveyance
- Operation, repair and maintenance of equipment
- Diesel, oil and lubricants (predominantly in construction projects)
- Travel
- Postal and telephone charges
- Finance costs
- Compliance on audit and statutory obligations
- Management supervision and other costs
- Taxes payable to government, excluding TDS and income tax.

Total costs

All these revenues and costs are prepared in table form and the difference in revenue and costs, positive or negative, are the monthly contributions to the organization from the project.

The owner conducts withdrawals from the project on the basis of this cash flow and arranges resources to mitigate negative cash flow.

Project cash flow is prepared at the start of the project and execution philosophy is planned to avoid negative cash flow to the project.

This could be achieved by completing good revenue-earning jobs early and mobilizing the project in a phased manner. Mobilization expenses are also given to the project based on this cash flow. The owner provides the means to cover negative cash flow beyond credits from suppliers, etc.

Difference between commercial performance and cash flow statements

Cash flow is the true projection of facts on how the money is moved in and out of the project under the responsibility of the project manager.

A commercial performance statement is prepared by the head office jointly with the project manager taking into account the following:

- Real profit or loss expected

- Status of in-house resources available and how much is to be charged to the project
- Statement of new assets to be procured and their utility to the company after the project is completed
- Extent of follow-up required by the head office
- Technical risks and their mitigation
- Logistical risks
- Political risks
- Quantity variations of work to be done on fixed-price projects
- Owner's contingency based on above risks
- Expected profits to be shown in balance sheet.

A performance statement would have the following cost heads:

Inflow

- Advances distributed, as planned, for each month
- Revenue/work bills for each month, as planned
- Less recovery of advances
- Less recovery of retention money, etc. from work bills
- Release of retention money by client

- TDS
- Net monthly inflow distributed for the project duration.

Outflow
Fixed costs

- Depreciation of equipment and other assets provided by the company, calculated at a monthly rate for each equipment/asset for the period of deployment*
- Project-specific equipment to be written-off on the project
- Purchase of know-how, consultant fees, computer programs, etc.
- Office and residential premise rentals
- Health, safety and environment costs
- Electricity, water and security
- Insurance
- Head office overheads, fixed per month for actual duration*** of project.

Variable costs, related to progress of work

- Procurement of consumables
- Salaries and wages
- Bonus and gratuities
- Incentives
- Cars and other conveyance

- Repair and maintenance of equipment
- Diesel, oil and lubricants (predominantly in construction projects)
- Travel
- Postal and telephone charges
- Finance costs
- Compliance on audit and statutory obligations
- Management direct supervision and other costs, including travel, for project
- Taxes payable to the government, excluding TDS and income tax
- Contingencies to be spent with the approval of the head office.

Total costs are the sum of fixed and variable costs

Statements of revenue and costs are prepared like cash flow statements and variance is reported to the head office.

MIS reporting should have both cash flow and performance statements with explanations for variances.

*All over the world, income tax authorities allow depreciation at 7–35 per cent of cost** of equipment and other assets, per year, at the choice of the owner since assets deteriorate/depreciate differently in different environments and working conditions. Further, this depreciation can be charged by the

straight-line method or on reducing balance at the discretion of the company.

** Capital cost could be considered in books of accounts as just the purchase price or inclusive of the following:

- Pre-dispatch inspection and testing
- Transport from manufacturing plant to the workplace
- Transit insurance
- Unloading from trucks and assembly
- Commissioning expenses, including cost of commissioning engineer's visit
- First fill of oil and lubricants.

*** Head office overheads are generally between 0.5 and 5 per cent of revenue. Some organizations escalate to even 8 per cent, but in such cases, they need to justify this to auditors.

A smart accountant will consider a high percentage of depreciation, straight-line method of calculating depreciation and only the purchase price as asset value to his advantage in performance reporting and balance sheet to show less profits and save on income tax. This builds enormous pressure on the project manager to somehow make profits for the owner, which is difficult unless the project has huge profit margins. In such cases, only cash flow statements come as rescue of the project manager.

The author once offered to quit in frustration, since for the three consecutive years in a new organization there were only losses in the balance sheet. The owner then explained that a trick had been employed. The owner continued to extract the last drop of sugarcane juice from the project manager for a good forty-three years of his association.

New project managers should take a lesson from this and be vigilant.

In India, on roadsides, there are small stalls where the shopkeeper crushes sugarcane sticks through two rollers to squeeze out the juice. He twists the residual sugarcane and puts it in the crusher, again and again, till he is satisfied that no more juice can be extracted and then throws away the crushed sugarcane fibers, good for burning.

Many Enterprise Resource Planning (ERP) packages are now available for computation of performance reports based on data fed into a computer as per clauses 3.2.2 to 3.2.4 and some other relevant data/considerations.

Basic parameters of the package should be understood by the project manager to avoid misguidance and his safety. Computers are slaves of executives, but we tend to become slaves of computers and accept any statement thrown out by the computer as correct, since we avoid analyzing

the computer program due to our incompetence or ignorance.

A computer programmer would ask similar questions to the project coordinator to prepare an ERP package and where information cannot be provided, would apply his/her own assumptions. With hardly any exception, these programs are owner-friendly, showing minimum possible profits for tax planning, paying dividends, etc., but remain unfair to the project manager. He gets the boot after slogging for a whole year. Hence, as stated earlier, the project manager should have basic checks of his own and the owner should know that this executive is aware of the tricks of the trade.

The owner of a construction company, in monthly reviews of progress, always ridiculed the chief executive for losses. At the same time, projects managers were showing good profits. One day, the frustrated chief executive shared with his managers the treatment he was getting from the owner. In the next meeting, the chief executive proposed to discuss reports prepared by his project managers. This statement was the end of the harassment since they did not want to face facts.

3.2.5 Health safety and environment protection compliances and achievements

Compliance with health, safety and environment protection regulations are important functions of any project and need to be addressed seriously even at the cost of progress of work or additional cost to the project. Implications of non-compliance could be serious in many ways, including the health and safety of workmen. If proper health care is not ensured, workers fall sick or are exhausted, which has serious implications on the progress of work.

Non-compliance of statutory requirements could have serious implications, with authorities taking action, disputes with workmen and a bad name for the organization. Hence, compliance with these requirements should be stringent and reported to the management through MIS in standard formats.

Landmark achievements of good health of workers and zero accident hours adds to the company's profile and brings appreciation for the project manager and his team.

3.2.6 Compliance with quality and standards and achievements

Good quality and workmanship have always been a major yardstick to check execution of any project. With technological advances, quality can be checked against well-documented and defined standards and their systems. It is a matter of interest and anxiety for both the client and the owner and they should be apprised of the effectiveness of quality compliance on a project; specific achievements could win praise. Hence, this must be a part of the MIS.

3.2.7 Further business prospects in the region

With everybody working so well and with good knowledge, the project manager should scout for new business with the same client or other clients in the vicinity. This would provide continuity of work or expansion of business in the same place. People would be willing to provide more work to performing contractors provided they do not become greedy and start quoting inflated rates. It is always counted in favor of a project manager if he gets more jobs due to good performance on the current job. Therefore, in his own interest, the project manager should have a column in his MIS for further business prospects to make management aware of such opportunities.

3.2.8 Any specific achievements

The owner is usually sitting away from the project location and would be delighted if the project has specific achievements. The project manager should not keep such achievements to himself and his team but share them with the owner, who will be happier to get such information directly from the project manager instead of a third party.

3.2.9 Any specific problems

It is not day-to-day problems that must be handled by the project team under the leadership of the project manager, but specific problems that may affect the project. When the project team does not have an appropriate solution, it should be highlighted to the owner through the MIS as well as direct communication with the owner's representative. Often, a project manager is questioned for not informing the owner about a major problem, since the latter might have solved it or suggested an alternative. The project manager's knowledge may not offer the best and ultimate solution to the problem. Further, if he informs the owner of such problems, the owner would be happy to share responsibility for setbacks if any.

3.3 Good Knowledge about the Project's Main Functions and Basic Knowledge of Its Support Functions

Unless the project manager has detailed knowledge of the main functions of the project, it is difficult for him to manage the project efficiently.

a. He has a team to execute the project but all his teammates need not be experts in their field of project execution. There will always be some who need guidance and control. If the project manager does not know how to execute the project, how can he guide others?

b. Even knowledgeable executives might get stuck due to an unforeseen problem. It is the duty of the project manager to help, guide and take decisions on execution methods to overcome such eventualities.

c. If the project manager avoids taking decisions, the executive might try to do the work to the best of his ability. If he succeeds, he gains appreciation but if he does not, it is the loss of the project manager. As the person responsible for the overall project, he is expected to solve all unforeseen problems.

d. If he is unable to solve problems, the project could start dragging, resulting in delays and extra costs, which may soon catch senior management's attention and they might lose confidence in his project-management abilities.

e. In the process, the project manager also loses the confidence and respect of his juniors. Executives who do well could become arrogant, damaging the harmonious working of the project.

f. The project manager should have basic knowledge of **support functions**, enough to read and understand their reports and requirements, connect the reports to project performance and discuss remedial measures to be taken.

g. Support functionaries are expected to be experts in their field and work under the guidance of and with the approval of the project manager. They are expected to explain a problem in detail, in layman's terms, to the project manager. For example, if there are cash flow problems, the finance manager must highlight these to the project manager, explain the problem in detail, suggest some solutions and then execute the solution agreed upon by everybody under his responsibility to project manager. The project manager is also responsible for the performance of the finance manager.

3.4 Dedication to Duty

The project manager is the owner's representative and does business on behalf of the owner. The only difference is that the owner gets full profit and may even make a loss in the business, but the project manager and his team gets their share in the expected profit, irrespective of profit or loss. **The project manager's actions, behavior and deliberations on different aspects and levels of the project are considered to be those of the owner.**

The project manager takes decisions on spending the money the owner has given in good faith. The owner gives the project manager the authority to spend this money as appropriate. Therefore, the project manager must be sincere and dedicated to his duty to perform all project activities in the best interests of the project and the owner. Only if the project manager himself is dedicated to his duty, can he expect similar dedication from his team.

3.5 Human Resource Management

On any project, human resource is the most important and sensitive resource in the command of the project manager. All the employees working on the project will work with confidence and interest if they are satisfied and feel that **someone** is taking care of issues like safety, health and working environments. This **someone** is the company and the project manager is the **company's representative**. He takes care of employees' welfare per the company's guidelines and policies with an initiative to implement such policies for a safe and comfortable working atmosphere.

The project manager must treat all the employees working with him equally, without any favors or consideration for relatives, friends, long association, caste, community, etc.

3.6 Planning and Foresight

All projects have a defined completion target. At the start of a project, the planning department, with the consent of the project manager, prepares a schedule for different activities in an expected sequence, mostly overlapping each other, with time allocated to each activity. This is called a project time schedule.

Once accepted, complying with this time schedule becomes the responsibility of the project manager. He owns the schedule and must complete the job within the specified time. He can reschedule activities as per prevailing situations and circumstances, but these must still be completed within the specified period.

The project manager should not blindly or in good faith accept the schedule but should study it thoroughly and ask the planning manager to explain each activity and make changes if necessary. Then, he and the planning manager must work out resources required to complete the project in time, requisition these from the management and seek instructions for mobilization.

This needs a good understanding of project execution for the whole period with reasonably **good foresight**. Resources required for different activities must be estimated correctly to prepare an efficient and workable time schedule.

It is easy to distribute all the activities between fixed start and finish times of the project. However, this is baseless and does not work in most cases.

Output parameters of skilled workers of different categories for all countries are available in books. Generally, overall efficiency is 70–80 per cent of theoretical efficiency and some contingencies are loaded on the resource requirement.

In November 1979, a project manager was requisitioned to take up a bad project, for PDO Oman in their oilfields, that had been dragging for three years with only 20 per cent work completed. The project contract conditions had a provision for unlimited liquidated damage recovery from the contractor for delays beyond the committed date of completion.

Liquidated damages had already accumulated to more than the net worth of the company. After studying the project in the field for a month, the project manager, with the consent of the general manager, opened his books to PDO and requested a waiver of liquidated damages if he completed the project in three months by March 10, 1980. This was accepted on the condition that if there was even a day's delay beyond March 10, PDO would have the right to charge full liquidated damages as per the contract.

The project manager prepared his work and resource schedules with 60 per cent contingencies and walked out on March 8, 1980, after handing over the project to the entire satisfaction of the client. In this period, there were two major accidents causing an average loss of two weeks of work and 10 days of unexpected delay in the supply of material in a three-month schedule. Some extra time and productivity was also lost in motivation and training human resources that had been idling for long. It takes a lot of effort and patience to restart a grinding wheel that has been idle for long. These contingencies cost a lot of money and should be planned judiciously as per the requirement of the contract. Generally, these contingencies are 5–15 per cent of the contract period.

It is essential that these schedules are prepared correctly. To do so, the project manager should understand the subject with reasonable foresight.

These schedules should be updated based on experience and the progress of the project, periodically, with related change of resources.

3.7 Cost Consensus

Any activity is carried out to serve some purpose Time, money and resources are spent on this activity. Quality of work and time spent are very important but at the same time, such costs should be affordable.

In 1976, a senior accounts manager fell from a motorcycle and sustained a fracture in his right arm. He went to an orthopedic surgeon to fix his hand. It was a time when fixing plates and rods through orthopedic surgery was new in India. The smart surgeon suggested two alternatives:

- He would fix the hand by setting the bones and putting a plaster cast on it for five weeks. This would be very cheap.
- He would open the affected area and fix a steel plate and the patient would be ready to work in four days. This would be very expensive.

For the patient, time and money as estimated by the surgeon were not as important as the quality and outcome of treatment. He also didn't think it was proper to unnecessarily spend company money by accepting the second alternative. The patient told the doctor, time was not a constraint as he did not want to spend unnecessary money but needed proper treatment for his hand to heal completely. If the doctor felt that the second alternative was unavoidable then he must choose that. While making a cost-based decision on either of the two alternatives was very much within his means, it was outside his capability to analyze which was better. He put his trust in the doctor and made him responsible for the cost and quality of the treatment.

The doctor arranged to conduct the treatment combining both alternatives and on a detailed investigation in the operation theater found that fixing the plate was necessary and did so after considering the cost implications of both the alternatives to the patient.

Being cost conscious is very important but quality and ultimate results should not be compromised.

3.8 Quality Conscious

If a project manager is quality conscious and does regular checks and provides tips for improving quality, subordinates also remain vigilant about maintaining good quality of work.

Providing consistently good quality of work is much appreciated and more intricate jobs are assigned to a performing project manager with good quality standards.

3.9 Negotiation Skills

3.9.1 Technical negotiations

A job can be executed in many ways depending on the situation, circumstances, related knowledge and availability of resources. The project manager is responsible for providing best possible quality results within the best possible time and costs. He must negotiate and discuss with the client's representative, vendors and even his subordinates and seniors on various technical matters to the satisfaction of all, in the best interests of the project.

A good negotiator is not one who impresses and somehow gets his views accepted by others. A good negotiator is one who understands the subject and with in-depth discussions finds a technical solution acceptable to him in the best interest of the project as agreed upon by all other participants in the discussion.

The project manager should place the proposal for discussion and have the concerned executive explain the merits and demerits. Everybody's views must be considered and discussed. The project manager should guide discussions in a constructive manner and a solution will emerge from these discussions. The final decision should be the project manager's since he is the leader of the team.

The project manager should not force his technical opinion on his subordinates without their understanding and acceptance otherwise they might not take any responsibility and in rare cases, even cause damage.

3.9.2 Commercial negotiations

Commercial negotiations with clients, vendors and others related to a project are an important part of the duties and responsibilities of a project manager.

For any procurement, different vendors provide prices, specifications, delivery parameters and warranties. The project manager and his team must skillfully negotiate with all vendors and get the best quality product at the least possible **price** and with satisfactory delivery and warranty parameters. Sometimes, a project manager delegates this responsibility to one of his juniors, but he must not have blind faith in anybody, including himself.

Senior management provides suggestions and advice but not instructions. The project manager must convince his boss about his proposal if he feels that the boss' proposal is not the best alternative.

The author worked directly under the owner of a company for more than 43 years. The owner always provided advice but never instructions on any technical or commercial matter. The author had many discussions with the owner on various issues. They convinced each other and the author executed all critical issues with the owner's agreement under his responsibility as the project manager.

3.10 Decision-Taking Abilities

Good knowledge on various work-related issues, analytical skills and self-confidence prompt a person to take a decision and own it in the event of a mistake.

It is not necessary to take a decision immediately, and wise executives buy time to communicate their decision. During this period, they think about various pros and cons and when satisfied that their decision is correct, communicate or implement the decision. Decision-takers are of the following types:

- One who takes a decision after comfortable analysis and owns the decision. He gets applause on a correct decision and suffers for wrong decisions.

- One who keeps changing his decisions, creating confusion and delays in the execution of his decisions.

- One who avoids taking decisions and makes someone else do it under his own responsibility. This person just provides his verbal consent.

Obviously, the person who takes and own his decisions is the more successful project manager. The person who does not take decisions gets exposed soon and keeps changing jobs. Many such people are very smart. They stay in an organization only for a short time but during this period they could harm some good executives, hence everybody should be cautious.

3.11 Emergencies and Crisis Management

Good emergency and crisis managers have the following qualities. They

- Do not become angry or nervous.
- Study and analyze the gravity of the situation quickly.
- Work out the maximum likely loss and retrieve the maximum possible.
- Ensure safe recovery of humans
  - By maintaining safety and ensuring that minimizing loss of life and injuries is top priority and
  - Arranging medical facilities.
- Divide crisis management resources into two parts: one that starts from retrieving the easiest possible subjects and ensuring the maximum possible number are saved easily and another that starts with the most difficult to retrieve subjects.
- Divert attention from what is already lost. Thus, teams and resources proceed and reach a comfortable meeting point.
- Simultaneously sound out the insurance company.
- Inform superiors.
- Prepare an action plan for the repair of partially damaged subjects.

- Prepare an action plan to replace completely damaged items.
- Formulate an overall habitation plan and its implementation schedule with estimates of additional resources, time and money required.
- Arrange resources to ensure a quick restoration to normalcy.
- Augment safety measures so such a crisis is not repeated.

The project manager and his team change priorities as the situation demands. The project manager should give a patient hearing to suggestions and implementation proposals by his teammates. This would induce better cohesive teamwork instead of a dictatorial atmosphere which may create chaos.

3.12 Team Building

3.12.1 For any organization and its project managers, team building is very important for the following reasons:

- Some senior executives leave the organization due to retirement.
- The organization needs more executives to handle an increase in business by taking on more projects.

- Every year, in addition to retiring executives, 10–30 per cent executives leave an organization for some reason or another.
- Trained and experienced executives at different levels are required to fill up the vacancies created due to above reasons.

3.12.2 It is always preferable to train and promote executives from within the organizational cadre instead of hiring new executives for the following reasons:

- Executives trained within the organization are conversant in the company's system and working style.
- Junior executives take more interest in learning since they can look forward to a good career.
- Junior executives become sincerer and the bond between employer and employee strengthens.
- The organization and the concerned project manager are aware of employees' strengths and weakness and placements are made accordingly.
- Due to proper and balanced placements at different levels on the project, the team is well-knit and collective efficiency is better.

A bonding develops between a trainer and a trainee and they prefer to work together, which the organization usually encourages, unless administrative problems could arise from such a relationship. Good employees should be retained even by going a little out of the way. Increments and promotions should be on merit and not on personal bias. Good health, safety and environment implementations help retain good employees.

The author was lucky enough to have the management authorize him to provide the best possible healthcare, hygienic food and good living environment to all his fellow employees and workers.

3.12.3 Hiring of senior executives has the following benefits and problems:

- By hiring some experienced and knowledgeable executives and training juniors under them, organizational capabilities and expertise increases.
- Old and trusted employees are deputed alongside these executives and they also learn new techniques.
- If the new executive is good and adaptable, he becomes an asset to the organization.
- A few who have self-confidence and courage to achieve desired results without fearing loss of job do very well and rise fast in a new organization provided they show honest results in a short time.

- Generally, good and well-trained executives rarely leave the organization nor does the organization let them go easily. Therefore, it is difficult to get best executives with specialization in any trade.

- It is difficult for an expert in a trade to adjust and adopt to a new working culture and administrative norms.

- Senior executives might encounter difficulties in adjusting to a new working environment and many leave in frustration after a few months. They might have enjoyed a free hand and enormous power in their previous job and could find hurdles in earning the trust of the new management quickly to exercise similar authority in their new assignments.

- It is difficult for the organization as well as the executive to adjust with each other.

- An executive who changes jobs frequently might not be the best and there might be hidden reasons for the changes.

- Often, if an efficient and well-admired executive leaves after years in an organization, he might have to change a few jobs and even settle down at a junior level.

Constraints described above can adversely affect the project/organization.

3.12.4 Under the circumstances explained above, it is always good to train employees and build a reliable and efficient team. Good, trusted employees should be sent for special short-term training courses to learn new techniques.

Some organizations draft a training calendar for each employee as per his job profile and it's mandatory to attend such training courses for eligibility for promotions. Expert consultants are also hired to guide and provide on-job training to all employees. This is a proven way to accrue additional expertise for the organization.

3.13 Presentable and Able to Converse with Clients and High-Profile People

The project manager is the representative of his company and must deal with and take vital decisions in consultation with clients and other high-profile people for the smooth running of the business and for getting new business.

- He should neither bow down too much nor accept all demands/requests by clients and visitors without receiving any visible consideration, otherwise such demands will keep increasing and become difficult to manage.

- He should not be nervous while talking with such people.

- He should discuss various issues politely, with a free mind, and should be able to convince others with his submissions and try to direct discussions to his advantage.

- He should not say **no** or **impossible**, but impress upon others the difficulty in accepting non-workable proposals.

- He should not annoy visitors and they should understand and accept his views and constraints.

- Additional work or change orders should have a price and he should politely state that such changes will have cost and time implications, which could be provided later after detailed computations.

- Similarly, for reduction in scope of work, a fair saving should be offered. It should not be one-way traffic for both parties.

- All discussions should be conducted keeping others on a reasonably high platform.

- If the project manager goes to the client's office, he will first encounter his assistant or peon; a small exchange of pleasantries helps move forward smoothly and quickly.

- His discussions should not be aggressive in any way or insulting to others and should always be polite.

- The project manager should be dressed well and as the situation demands. If he travels to meet clients, they will note his attire, presentation, the car he travels in and the hotel he stays in. They will offer a meeting in their office at their time or in the project manager's hotel at his convenience. Both have lot of differences in approach and meeting atmosphere, in favor of or against the visiting executive and shows how others assess his importance.

- Project manager should provide/create a meeting environment conducive to status of visiting guest.

An old, blind man was trying to sleep on the footpath on a cold night. A king passed by and sent a blanket with his peon for him. The peon went with the blanket and said, "Hey, beggar, the king has sent a blanket for you. Cover yourself and sleep well." The blind man refused to take the blanket. Then, the king sent his minister with the blanket. The minister said, "I have brought a blanket for you. This will protect you from freezing cold." The blind man again refused. The king then went himself and said, "My dear friend, this blanket will ensure you don't fall sick on this cold night.

Kindly accept it. I would be obliged." The old, blind man recognized the king, stood up and thanked the king with folded hands and prayed for him.

How you speak and present yourself makes a lot of difference and impact. A project manager is a king but he must earn respect and retain his chair by his behavior and produce desired results in his assignments and career.

4.0

Some Management Stories

1. Innovation
2. Planning
3. Emphasis on human resource development
4. Keeping abreast of the latest updates, conducting workshops frequently to keep the team updated with the latest advances
5. Pricing
6. Relationship with subordinates
7. Distribution of duties to juniors and making them responsible for it
8. Relationship with colleagues
9. Relationship with superiors

10. Importance of controlling stress and avoiding work fatigue
11. Public relations
12. Quality assurance
13. Health, safety and environment
14. Business development
15. Hierarchy
16. Incentive

4.1 Innovation

The sales promotion committee of a toothpaste manufacturer were in a conference hall, debating how to increase the sales of their product. They already had more than 85 per cent market share. Some innovative idea needed to be coined to further increase in sales. Senior executives could not find a solution. A waiter serving them tea overheard their conversation. He suggested that satisfaction in using a toothpaste from the tube comes from the length of the paste on the toothbrush and not the quantity. If the size of the hole in the tube was increased, consumption would increase.

A person sitting under a tree and seeing a fruit fall put forward the theory of gravitational force which allows the earth to pull everything towards itself and ensures we don't fly off or are hurt by strong winds.

A person who felt lighter while sitting in his bathtub full of water invented floatation, the concept of objects floating in water.

Mahatma Gandhi invented and successfully used the tool of non-violence to fight mighty governments in Africa and then in India.

Innovative concepts seem like common sense in day-to-day life, but their application may need some technical knowledge. These concepts emerge from some innovative ideas through a serious thought process in different situations in everybody's life.

Getting a project is very easy but its implementation through to successful completion is always a challenge. During the implementation of a project, many unexpected situations may arise and in such cases, people look to the person who can solve problems with innovative solutions.

Such skills and knowledge are not God's gift but are developed if one takes interest in one's work and works hard to solve ticklish problems. Results must and do emerge. Once you solve a problem, you get motivated. You then take interest, with confidence, in solving more problems and the process continues, making your work easier and you are chosen to take on bigger challenges. This is how one gets recognized and one's progress graph becomes steeper.

Many project managers are very innovative while others keep innovative persons around and look after them very well.

There are many consulting companies, providing consultancy on how to handle a ticklish job. They become very popular in a short time and earn a big name and money.

The captain of a sports team would prefer the players in his team to be able to play in different adverse situations with innovative skills. **They are project managers of their own little but important projects.**

4.2 Planning

An American multinational company was awarded a license/permission to extract petroleum gas from a place in a deep forest that had hostile tribes and was about 800 km from the closest port. This project changed hands thrice among American majors due to logistics and other difficulties and remained a non-starter for many years.

The company that successfully executed the project built an airport, at their own cost, to fly in from the sea port about 100 loads of oilfield equipment, with each load weighing about 400 tons. This was done using the biggest cargo aircraft in the world with the best safety and operational standards. The airport was completed in three and a half years and equipment was brought to the site ahead of schedule.

In the implementation stage, the planning group understood the gravity of the task ahead and planned the project as under:

- Contract for construction was given to a group of three multinational companies from Australia, Greece and India. The Indian company was a subcontractor with the understanding that all three would complement each other and in case any one company lagged, the others would step in.

- Resources were mobilized to complete the job in 18 months on a three-and-a-half-year schedule, that is, more than 100 per cent contingency in resources and time for project completion.

- Men, material and construction equipment for this airport, including oil well drilling equipment, were airlifted by smaller aircrafts to the nearest airstrip by chartered aircrafts and a series of helicopters provided by the client.

- The contractor temporarily upgraded forty kilometers of road, from an existing small airstrip to the project site to supplement the work of the helicopters, and provide road transport for men, materials and equipment.

- Since this road had frequent landslides, even diesel and food were airlifted by helicopters while the road was being repaired.

- For safety on the road, check posts were set up at strategic locations and traffic assistants were posted at sharp and difficult bends on the road.
- Each truck load moved with two escort vehicles to carry out emergency breakdown repairs, safeguard material against theft and easily navigate sharp bends, including steep slopes. Additional vehicles were provided to pull loaded trucks on difficult slopes.
- The site had a malarial mosquito menace. Mosquito-repellent was regularly sprayed on the entire site and its surroundings during the entire period of construction and operations. In addition, daily anti-malarial pills were mandatory for all those working on the project.
- A full-fledged dispensary was set up at the site.
- A water-treatment plant, its trunk lines and sewage treatment plants were the first to be installed at the site.

The airport was completed in three and a half years at 25 per cent of the time and cost of the original plan for upgrading an 800 km road connecting the sea port to the site through steep mountains and thick forests.

This is an example of good, innovative, far-sighted planning, other companies could not think about.

Planning is an important function of every project. It is a detailed estimation of how and when a job will be executed in different stages. Plans are always written down and upgraded by repeated reading and thinking before work starts and during implementation.

There is an old saying: a tree can be cut in a planned manner in one hour while it takes twice the time and effort to cut it in an unplanned manner. In cutting the tree in a planned manner, the axe is sharpened after every few strokes, depending on the hardness of timber. In the other case, one keeps striking with a blunt axe, hardly able to cut the tree.

4.3 Emphasis on Human Resource Development

People arrive at a certain stage of expertise not just through their own efforts, but in addition mostly due to contributions of their trainers. Success is not achieved by mere classroom training; in most cases, it is achieved by someone providing an opportunity to work and grow under his guidance. This is the development of a human resource.

Similarly, a project manager and his team must contribute well to the training and development of freshers in the team as a moral responsibility as well in the interest of their own development. Knowledge always increases when it is shared.

At the age of seventy-three, the author is still learning by sharing his knowledge. New ideas and concepts keep emerging and it is very interesting and refreshing to share with pleasure. This is the real prize for producing books like this one.

If a project manager trains a team of fresh personnel, the team is groomed as per his expectations and style of working. This makes the job simple, the workplace more comfortable with good understanding and the work is of better quality with minimum effort.

A good statue can be made with wet clay (young people); one can shape it the way one likes. However, if someone tries to make a statue out of hard clay, it will break, unless it is softened first, which is always a pleasure but sometimes difficult.

It is an old saying that one gets good trees and fruits from good seeds, depending on the way they are sown and grown. Good seeds do not always give good fruits. A person has a big plot of land that he puts to use for horticulture. He plans what to grow depending upon the

- nature of the soil
- weather conditions
- market demand
- expertise
- resources like humans, water, power, connectivity with marketplace, etc.

Then, he selects seeds as per his requirement and taste. Sowing seeds in the ground is not enough. For seeds to produce healthy plants, they need to be nurtured by protecting them from storms, rain and heat, and providing manure at different stages. Ultimately, with a lot of continuous and dedicated attention, seeds grow into strong and healthy trees that bear fruits that the owner desires.

Similarly, project managers often get a project that is like barren land. They must develop their own human resources, with different skills as per their requirement, to work with them on the project. Ultimately, they produce a team ready to execute other projects as well after the completion of the current project. This is also good support for organizational team building.

For a project in a very remote area, only a few experts were brought in and 85 per cent of the workforce was made up of raw hands who learnt new skills through on-job training.

All senior executives have a responsibility to develop more executives capable of giving good performance. This is necessary for the growth of a senior executive in his organization, for his own satisfaction and for gaining the respect of juniors.

As a moral responsibility to society, every successful individual should provide training to, if not many, at least one person. He should groom this person and pass on all the knowledge nature has bestowed on him. **Knowledge should not die with a person.**

Emperor ShahJahan cruelly cut off one hand of all the workers who built the Taj Mahal, so that another such monument would not be built. Good and difficult art and skills have died again and again with the passage of time. This is an irretrievable loss to mankind. **Our world would have been different if knowledge and skills were properly preserved, continuously upgraded and recorded. Today, it is difficult to build seven wonders despite our so-called technological advances. It is regrettable that innovative concepts were not preserved.**

4.4 Keeping Abreast of the Latest Updates, Conducting Workshops Frequently to Keep the Team Updated with the Latest Advances

All over the world, in different walks of life, continuous development is taking place in all fields as a matter of routine; without this, humans could not have achieved the present state of development. It is important to be aware of the latest developments in one's field of expertise and implement them in one's profession with the possibility of further upgradation as a responsibility. This helps to improve work and growth in the profession.

Many organizations maintain a separate team of experts to collect the latest news on technological advances and filter them to make them relevant to the company's interest and growth. Workshops and training programs are planned with experts who are knowledgeable about such developments, so employees can understand and implement these for their own growth and that of the organization.

In many cases, promotions are denied if an employee does not attend such short-term courses on the pretext of being very busy at work; one's work can be seconded to someone for a while.

Sometimes, for the implementation of new technology on a specific project, it is considered advantageous to bring in experts to guide and teach a group of employees working on the project and conduct frequent classroom sessions. This helps in the following ways:

- Work starts early and progress is not interrupted.
- Knowledge is transferred to a group of people and not an individual.
- All related employees learn the technology while working.
- Most problems and doubts are resolved before the expert leaves the organization.
- The organization and employees gain more expertise.

This is how a developing company and the country grow in different fields of expertise and slowly become self-reliant in many types of skills/technologies.

Japan is an example. It learnt technology from the west, improvised and soon became a world leader in technology. For some time, Japanese experts were discouraged from going to Germany, they would learn to manufacture just by seeing some products. Now, they are opening industries in underdeveloped countries to hire cheap labor, train them and produce high-grade equipment for exports.

In post-independence India, even wheat was imported from the United States. Agriculturists learnt better technology from other countries and implemented in India. Simultaneously, the country improved irrigation, fertilizer production, tools and equipment resources. India became self-reliant in food products despite population growth. India now exports food products. India is now a world leader in many fields and exports technology to other countries.

All this is possible by keeping abreast of the latest updates and conducting workshops frequently to keep teams equipped with the latest advances.

4.5 Pricing (in Major Contracts for Execution of a Project)

There is a difference between the cost and the price of a project. Cost is what is estimated to be spent and price is the amount of money to be charged to the customer. This is well understood but all items of work may not necessarily have a uniform markup on cost to arrive at the price. Money spent for fixed costs like, overheads, markup, contribution, profits, etc. is distributed to direct costs of all the items based on many considerations, including:

- pricing to support cash flow
- balanced pricing
- aggressive pricing
- pricing related to performance

Pricing to support cash flow

An entrepreneur never does business with his own money. At best, he would create basic infrastructure, employ a few experts and provide for their salaries for a few months.

Someone intending to start a business would hire a well-known person in the industry as his project manager with some support staff. Then, they would prepare an impressive presentation showing the capabilities of the project manager and themselves. If an impressive office is not available, a suite in a good hotel could be hired as an office and start scouting for business.

On approval of a project by concerned authorities, money will be needed to start the business. There is a system of getting an advance payment by providing a bank guarantee to the customer. The bank would provide a guarantee only when immovable assets free of any encumbrances are pledged. This is difficult for any organization in the initial stages of business and even if feasible, should be avoided.

To circumvent this problem, a major portion of the fixed costs to be spent in the initial stages of the project are charged to the project as items of works in the billing schedule and the rest of the fixed costs are spread equally to all direct costs of items in the billing schedule. These billing items for fixed costs are covered under widely acceptable additional heads in the billing schedule called **preliminaries**. These could generally be charges in sub heads as

- Mobilization of project manager
- Office space
- Equipment mobilization
- Providing insurance policy
- Providing bank guarantees as per contract

A few more similar project-specific items of work could be added.

Towards the end of 1979, the author was interviewed for a senior position in Oman. Only one question was asked, "Why should we appoint you?" The author replied, "I fry fish with its own oil" and was selected. The company was in bad shape and within three years, the new team turned the company into a profit-making organization.

One puts fish on the frying pan and heats it slowly. A little later, the fish starts releasing its own oil. Keep frying the fish as this oil is released. This strategy could be used for starting many new projects in all fields, by preparing smart pricing schedules. The project manager keeps getting paid for all expenses in the initial stages of the project and does not need any advances. This also keeps the customer comfortable since some progress is visible as money is spent.

Cash inflow should always be more than outflow through smart pricing for the project in initial stages.

Balanced pricing

In the above pricing module, after reducing amounts charged for preliminaries, the remaining amount of fixed cost is distributed evenly to all the direct costs in the billing schedule, without changing the overall price. This is balanced pricing.

This is the normal way to price a project and the contractor does not lose or gain much due to fluctuations in scope of work. He just gets at the rate of actuals on increase or reduction in scope. His profits also increase or decrease accordingly.

However, instead of evenly distributing fixed costs on billing items, placing some fixed costs on monthly instalments is a good option.

- If a job duration is increased due to delays in client decision making, the client does not mind paying fixed costs being billed on a monthly basis for an extended period.

- If the scope is reduced with reduction in time, the contractor does not lose, since only fixed costs of establishment salaries, etc. for the reduced scope of work is reduced, which the contractor would not spend now.

- If the scope of work increases without a time extension, the contractor would not get profits on extended scope, since only direct costs would be reimbursed. In such cases, try to get extra fixed costs since additional resources would be needed to do more work in the same time, which should be added to fixed monthly costs.

Aggressive pricing

Aggressive pricing is dangerous; it could benefit the project manager but could also cause heavy losses. Hence, it should be done carefully, with the consent of superiors.

Aggressive pricing could be done in two ways:

- Front loading
- Strategic loading

Front loading

Front loading is done to further improve cash inflow. In addition to preliminaries, in the initial stages of the project, prices of items to be completed first are increased and correspondingly prices for items to be completed at the end of the project are reduced. The owner takes away his profit and the fate of the project is left in the hands of the project manager and his team and often, even survival becomes difficult. The project begins to drag and fixed costs increase, resulting in losses to the project. Therefore, front loading should be conservative to the extent that cash flow is workable up to the end even if the owner takes away surplus cash in the initial stages of the project.

On most projects, the client is very liberal in making payments in the initial stages. He has enough money at that time and he wants the contractor to be happy and take an interest in the project. As the project proceeds, cash balance in hand decreases and as extra work is to be executed at the client's insistence, he becomes stingy and starts delaying project payments. Hence, it is in the interest of the contractor to pick up his profits as soon as possible.

After the Indo-China war in 1962, the Government of India had a cash crunch and it took some time for the economy to pick up. Many defense projects were picked up on priority by the government and money to be spent on ongoing civil projects was diverted to defense projects.

A road bridge was being built on a big river in North India and the government was unable to fulfil its financial commitments on time. The government called the contractor for a meeting, where the contractor proposed three alternatives:

- Stop the work temporarily. Contractor would demobilize his resources, complete other important work and come again when the government called, to complete the bridge. The government would pay the cost for demobilization and remobilization of resources as per the conditions of the contract.

- Stop the work and cancel the job on an as-is and where-is basis with mutual consent. This would be good for the contractor since he had already lifted his profit.

- Continue the work with normal progress and the government would somehow arrange funds. As a goodwill gesture, the contractor would accept reasonable delays in payments.

This is how front loading helps. In most cases, the contractor diverts money to other projects and a project may suffer due to money shortage towards the end. Hence, front loading should always be within limits and enough provisions should be left to complete the work on time from accruals of the project, without asking for money from the owner.

Strategic loading

Once the structure of pricing is ready, generally it goes to the project manager for final fine-tuning. Every project manager has a strategy for how and when he would deliver different stages/milestones on the project. He also speculates on grey areas where there is a scope for increase or decrease in the quantity of work. Accordingly, he changes some numbers by increasing and decreasing prices for different items, keeping the total price the same or even reduce with no change in commitments of profits.

This helps in increasing the ultimate price of the project if the scope of work of the selected items is increased. In case of reversal, he could make a loss. Hence, strategic loading should be discouraged. In case of reversal, it becomes difficult to convince management. After all, on the other side of table are intelligent people also looking to protect their interests.

On an airport construction project, a temporary shelter for aircrafts was to be built as a lumpsum item and no permanent shelter was planned. The contractor heavily loaded the price of this item. The client cancelled this item after awarding the contract. However, the contractor was paid a small but reasonable sum to compensate loss in profit for deleting this item after long deliberations.

For the construction of a major port, a substantial quantity of hard rock was to be blasted under water and removed. However, the client, without understanding the seabed profile, estimated a small amount for rock removal. An intelligent project manager took a quick physical check at the site and on confirmation of his expectations, put a high price for this item and reduced the quoted price. This tilted the decision on the award of the contract in his favor and he made a higher-than-expected profit due to the considerable increase in the quantities of rock blasting.

Pricing related to performance

In the software industry, many operating business houses in different trades give contracts to software companies to develop Enterprise Resource Planning (ERP) software or similar packages suitable for their business. Such contracts involve many innovations and the product is unique and suitable for the business. The quality of the product is most important and orders are placed based on past performances. Such projects are high-value jobs and a substantial amount is held back for a few months until the successful operation of the package/system.

In one construction project, due to lagging past experience, the client ignored the lowest bidder and intended to give the contract to the second lowest bidder at a higher price. The lowest bidder offered to take the payment in full only after successful completion of the project and took away the contract.

Even for senior executives in coveted positions, the annual pay package is divided into two parts and 30–50 per cent of their salary is kept on hold and released only on successful performance in the appraisal period. This system is called Annual Performance-Linked Incentive (APLI). On satisfactory performance, the executive gets the full amount of the agreed APLI and on extraordinary performance, this amount can even be doubled. In case of unsatisfactory performance, APLI is not paid for that year.

4.6 Relationship with Subordinates

For a project manager, his subordinates are his biggest resource. Without the cooperation and active involvement of his team mates, that is, his subordinates, the project manager cannot achieve good output and progress. He should be fair with all subordinates and treat preferred subordinates more strictly.

A project manager is also expected to help all subordinates develop in their respective trades and specializations to become good project managers as soon as possible. Training should not be just job-specific but should aim for overall improvement in understanding different concepts of the trade.

Professionals or parents are successful when they are introduced as teachers or parents of a successful individual. The greatest satisfaction is seeing one's disciple doing better than oneself.

Mohan Rao was working well as a senior engineer with his boss for some time. The boss recommended that Mohan be a project manager on a large project. Mohan asked for his boss's guidance in project planning. The boss scolded him, saying that if he could not do the planning, he was not worthy of being called the boss' student. Mohan took this as a challenge and the project was ultimately completed a few days before time and at the cost he had projected. He got an appreciation letter from the owner of the company.

In a different case, the management of a company, at the discretion of the concerned project managers, announced an incentive of one month's salary for one or two employees who proved to be good performers. A project manager arranged a get-together in the evening for all employees with their families. In this gathering, he announced the names of two employees who had performed well, with a detailed account of their performance. This was good motivation for all employees to perform better in future and the decision was unanimously endorsed. It was a very difficult task for the project manager to choose best performers from a large team, correctly and honestly, without favoring any one and in a manner acceptable to all colleagues.

4.7 Distribution of Duties to Juniors and Making Them Responsible for It

A renowned politician was sworn in as the prime minister of a country and enjoyed his full term of five years. He selected his ministers very carefully, from among the best available in different professions and made them accountable for their portfolios. These ministers managed the functioning of their departments to the best of their ability under the prime minister's leadership. A few were also changed for unsatisfactory performance while better portfolios were given for good performance. The prime minister was always present in parliament and patiently heard all conversations, but avoided speaking and managed his business by directing his ministers to take the lead.

The prime minister completed his tenure of five years with the help of his ministers but, probably because his personal contribution was not visible, this marked the end of his political career. His party lost heavily in the next general elections, possibly because of their choice of prime ministerial candidate.

Delegation of duty to juniors is good but must be within certain limits and the organization should also be able to see positive personal contributions and not just a figurehead.

4.8 Relationship with Colleagues

The relationship with colleagues must be cordial and help must be provided to each other as per circumstances. It should not be one-way traffic of giving or taking. Senior colleagues should help their juniors, who should, in turn, respect and listen to their seniors and provide support when required.

4.9 Relationship with Seniors

The author was placed under a freshly recruited senior executive for some time for a very specialized task: heavy rock blasting using more than a ton of explosives per day. After a few months, due to the exigencies and requirements of the project, the assignment was split and the senior executive was requested to devote more time on a difficult portion of the job and the author was given independent charge for his portion of the work. Soon, something went wrong and the senior executive politely refused to take any responsibility for the author's work since he was not being consulted. This was the end of the so-called independent charge on that project for the author.

The author should have maintained good relationship with his senior, who taught him the trade and consulted the senior in cases of difficulties.

Seniors are more knowledgeable and are not in any way competing with their juniors. Therefore, they could provide good support in case of need, if approached respectfully.

It was not mandatory for the senior executive to part with his knowledge to his juniors. The author must have kept him in the same elevated status as before.

There is a difference between a teacher and a tutor. A tutor imparts knowledge for a consideration and only to the extent that is required for the purpose, while a teacher teaches a subject in-depth, ensuring that the student has understood it well and is able to further implement it, as and when required. This knowledge sharing does not have a price tag.

4.10 Importance of Controlling Stress and Avoiding Work Fatigue

All humans have a level of stamina for comfortable exertion. After this level, they are working under stress and soon they reach the stage of fatigue, the stage of giving up.

Once in a while, working up to the stress level should be all right, but this should not be a routine or frequent affair. Reaching this level of fatigue affects work and health and must be avoided. Regular breaks for rest and entertainment should be planned for all workers at all levels, including the project manager himself, to divert their minds from work. This helps the brain and body relax. The brain never sleeps, but by changing the subject of thought and the operations of the brain, the portion of the brain that is working goes into rest mode. This helps ensure good health, concentration on job and better productivity. A change could include playing, shopping, entertainment and even going to sleep for a while. A mid-day break with about 30 minutes' sleep after lunch makes executives fresh for another five to six hours of work.

Similarly, it is also necessary that the body relaxes after working for long and getting tired. **This is also applicable to animals.** When a lion gets tired of running during a hunt, it stops and relaxes for a while even at the cost of losing its prey.

The donkey is generally considered lacking in intelligence, an animal that keeps working as per the requirements of its master. This is a **misunderstanding**. A donkey works as labor and has a mental clock. It stops working after its normal working schedule. If it has had eight to ten hours work by 3 pm, it will stop work at three and will not work further, irrespective of how much the master beats it.

Donkeys keep walking between the loading and unloading points shown by the master the whole day, without break, using the shortest and safest route and will not accept overloading. They will shake their bodies and throw off the excess load.

Many organizations no longer allow encashment of leaves or carrying forward of balance leave and all employees are required to take leave to refresh themselves.

Work does not suffer due to the absence of anybody if the work is explained well to subordinates and colleagues before proceeding on leave. If a person does not explain his work properly, it could be bad for his career.

A successful manager should not be surprised if his team is more productive in his absence, since they feel more responsible. This is good management and the manager gets credit for the efficient working of his team and even gets quick promotions.

This is a test management usually applies before transferring a senior employee to a new assignment: seeing how his team performs in his absence.

4.11 Public Relations

Most projects are planned and executed in public interest. Projects are rarely far from habitation and the public is affected directly or indirectly. Public participation should be welcome. People would be curious about what is happening and a few are interested in knowing and understanding the outcome of a project. Often, they might give suggestions that might be innovative and good. Their suggestions must be understood, expanded upon and implemented for the betterment of the project.

Even in household affairs, a good rapport with neighbors and the surrounding society provides good dividends.

A project manager gets a free consultant with innovative ideas for the benefit of the project that he will get credit for and the public feels good and thus becomes more cooperative. The project manager also gets a new friend and improves his own image in public.

A shoe-manufacturing company sent their sales representative to a tribal area to ascertain the scope of selling shoes in the area. He returned after a few days and submitted that there was no scope since nobody wore shoes.

After some time, another representative was sent to the same place to find out if there was any scope to sell shoes. He returned with a report that there was excellent scope and even a new factory could be opened in the area. With good public relations, the people could be taught to wear shoes. Once shoes were found to be comfortable, everybody would start wearing them. This sales representative was promoted and made project manager for the area, where everybody started wearing shoes and blessed the project manager for adding comfort to their life.

4.12 Quality Assurance

It does not cost much to do a quality job. Bad quality generally cannot be repaired to match good quality product. A quality job just needs willpower, concentration and frequent checks during execution.

It is not proper to blame knowledge; if one does not have adequate knowledge, it is impossible to do even a bad job. Application of knowledge with the intention of doing a good job is necessary; it may just take more time and concentration.

If a bad job is done and not accepted, cost and time to repair the bad job is far greater than the extra time spent in doing a good job. Also, repair is always repair and never matches a good job done at first instance.

All manufacturers of automobiles and household appliances give one or two years' warranty. Customers do not buy these items just for one or two years; they expect long-lasting performance. Hence, they conduct a market survey on the performance of different brands and then purchase the best-performing product, one that provides better quality, durability and the least maintenance even at some extra cost.

Hence, maintaining good quality praises the project manager first and then the customer.

4.13 Health, Safety and Environment

4.13.1 Health

Maintenance of good health is important for well-being and efficient working. It is cheaper to arrange health care in-house by appointing a part-time doctor or a dispensary to take care of the health-related problems of all employees. This increases productivity and interest in the job while reduces absenteeism, good for the project.

4.13.2 Safety

Safety of men, equipment and materials must be of prime importance on any project. Safe working ensures greater confidence, better productivity and lesser overall costs. Safety breaches occur through small mistakes and ignorance. The entire team including the project manager should have regular safety briefings by experts related to the project.

4.13.3 Environment

Environment protection has always been a high priority and is now the need of the day for the whole world. Life on this planet is possible because we get good air with enough oxygen to breathe, a comfortable atmospheric temperature, water, food and light — the basic requirements for the existence of life. There is also a natural system for recycling consumables and waste, maintaining a balance in environmental facilities.

Due to an increasing population and the corresponding exploitation that is manifested in the cutting of forests, the neglecting of air and ground pollution and the depleting of the groundwater table, etc. environmental balance is at risk. Already, temperatures have started rising and might reach a level harmful for life in the long run. Hence, it is the duty of all humans to be environment friendly and try and protect natural assets by:

- Controlling air pollution created through various sources.
- Controlling vehicular emission through regular and proper maintenance and minimizing the use of vehicles.
- Avoiding cutting trees and planting many trees when one is cut. All governments have regulations to be followed for cutting trees.

- Avoiding heavy deforestation that disturbs the ecological balance of a region.
- Covering trucks loaded with loose earth, coal, etc. so that no pieces can fall off fast-moving vehicles and damage other vehicles, injure people, affect cleanliness of roads or create dust.
- Disposing waste after proper treatment as per government norms.
- Maintaining hygiene for sanitation and disposing sewage after proper treatment.
- Harvesting rain water.
- Ensuring surface water drainage and subsidence.
- Minimizing exploitation of subsoil water and avoiding wastage.
- Controlling sound pollution and unnecessary honking and other loud noises.
- Maintaining social harmony through pleasant and disciplined actions.

The importance of a resource is felt only when it is in short supply. Why not avoid short supply by judiciously using natural resources?

Singapore is using water from sewage treatment plants for drinking and recycling as much water as possible through mechanical means. Other nations should take a lesson from this.

In Oman, drinking water is produced by treating sea water, through a process called desalination, because little ground water is available. Desalination is viable only in countries where fuel, like natural gas, is cheaply available in abundance.

Even the discharge of pure hot water into the sea is a deterrent to marine life. Treated hot water from industries is discharged in the deep sea, about half a kilometer away from the sea shore at the minimum possible temperature with a built-in sprinkler so that it mixes instantaneously with large volumes of sea water, thus reducing the speed of water discharge and the effect of a higher temperature on marine life.

4.14 Business Development

Progress is important on a continuous basis for any successful individual. As stated earlier, without continuous progress, humans would not have reached where they have. **Satisfaction** and **impossible** are not in the dictionary of successful individuals. Progress stops once you are satisfied or feel that further progress in any field is not possible. It means you have arrived at your saturation and retirement stage.

A project manager should always be on the lookout in his surroundings and beyond for add-ons to his business for his personal and organizational growth. He should tap all opportunities, although he might not achieve success in all efforts.

4.15 Hierarchy

A project manager must respect his superiors and listen to their advice. In case of disagreement, concerns should be sorted through detailed discussions. He must not disobey his immediate superior, which may have adverse repercussions. The project manager will also expect similar treatment from his juniors.

4.16 Incentive

Incentive to work is a good and successful tool for good work and progress for all. A project manager and his team should always have a goal to achieve and it is the duty of the project manager to set up such goals for his team and have certain benefits from success. Such benefits are called incentives.

Incentives could be of many types including

- self-satisfaction
- appreciation
- throwing a party
- better job opportunities, including training
- a holiday break
- promotion
- gifts
- monetary benefits.

Wishing readers all the best in their profession and life,

Prem Vardhan

www.ingramcontent.com/pod-product-compliance
Lightning Source LLC
Chambersburg PA
CBHW020446220526
45464CB00002B/879